small kid time hawaii

edited by Eric Chock

Bamboo Ridge Press
1981

ISBN 0-910043-03-5

Bamboo Ridge Press is a nonprofit, tax-exempt corporation formed in 1978 to foster the appreciation, understanding, and creation of literary, visual, or performing arts by, for, or about Hawaii's people. This book was funded in part by grants from the State Foundation on Culture and the Arts (SFCA) and the Coordinating Council of Literary Magazines. The SFCA is funded by appropriations from the Hawaiʻi State Legislature and by grants from the National Endowments for the Arts.

Bamboo Ridge is published twice a year. For subscription information, back issues, or a catalog, please contact:

Bamboo Ridge Press
P.O. Box 61781
Honolulu, HI 96839-1781
(808) 626-1481
brinfo@bambooridge.com
www.bambooridge.com

Editors: Eric Chock and Darrell H.Y. Lum
Graphics & Design: Darrell H.Y. Lum
Cover: Grant Kagimoto, Cane Haul Road Ltd.

Every effort has been made to reach the students whose poems appear in this book. In some cases, this has proved unsuccessful. The publishers will be glad to hear from any such student.

10 9 8 7 6 5   00 01 02 03 04 05

Table of Contents

PREFACE

One of the pleasures of being a poet in Hawaii is meeting with students to talk about what a poet is and what poetry means to me. The joy comes from showing them how poetry can be a meaningful experience for them too, and from the poems they write in response to my brief visits with them. Most of the poems in this book were written by 8 to 12 year old public school children, with a sprinkling of poems by intermediate and high school students. I would like to express my thanks to them for keeping poetry alive and well in Hawaii. I only regret that so many other poems could not also be included.

To every one of you, "Thanks eh. See you around."

I would also like to acknowledge the Poets In The Schools project, co-sponsored by the Department of Education and the State Foundation on Culture and the Arts, with support from the National Endowment for the Arts, a federal agency. Since the 1973-74 school year I have been a participant in the P.I.T.S., under whose auspices most of my class visits were made. My sincerest appreciation to all the administrators, principals, and teachers who made my class visits possible.

Introduction: What Can I Say?

I.

When I make my visits to the schools, students, teachers, and administrators are somewhat skeptical of me, a long-haired local guy who is supposed to be a poet. It seems that most people have never met a practicing poet, and they don't know what to expect.

At one school I visited I knew that they expected little, because I was told from the start that "*our* kids aren't very interested in poetry." In addition, they gave me their lower achieving levels of 4th, 5th, and 6th graders, as if testing my insistence that their reading and writing abilities didn't matter to me.

As it turned out, the kids were more interested in poetry than many of my other classes, especially when they found out I was sincerely interested in their thoughts and feelings being creatively expressed, no matter how ungrammatical or misspelled the initial drafts might have been. Once they realized it was a game played with the imagination more than with the pencil, poetry became enjoyable. The teachers were duly impressed with their students' performances, echoing a comment frequently heard, "So-and-so surprised me, I didn't know he was capable of expressing such ideas and feelings! I didn't know he could write like that!"

So on my last day I was feeling good as I walked out of the building. As I was about to go through the doorway I heard a man's voice behind me,"Eh STOP! Who're you?"

I turned around and saw a man with a shirt and tie looking

at me. "I'm Eric Chock, the Poet in the School," I said, a bit scared by the loud voice. I held my books up so he could see them.

"Ohh, ohh..." he replied. "I heard about you. They said you were doing good things with our students. They said they were writing some interesting things. I'm the principal. Pleased to meet you."

He shook my hand, and looking at me, he continued. "You know," he said, "I didn't recognize you cause you have such long hair. I thought only artists had long hair. I didn't know poets could have long hair too."

We both broke out laughing. I was flabbergasted and didn't know what to say.

What I wanted to say was that poets are artists too, like musicians, actors, dancers, and graphic artists, but instead of painting pictures with paints they use words. Instead of using their bodies or musical instruments to express their thoughts and feelings, they try to make a direct communication from mind to mind, heart to heart, with words.

And this is what I tell them on the first day.

The idea that poets can't have long hair reveals a commonly held prejudice that poets are scholars and intellectuals more than they are artists; that they are esoteric philosophers not interested in varieties of beauty as seen from the human point of view; that few people can really understand poetry.

This misunderstanding of poets and poetry is being passed on to our chldren. One of the primary values of arranging classroom visits by practicing poets who reside in the area is to afford students the opportunity to understand for themselves what poets and poetry is really about.

II.

One of the main things I try to do when I visit a school is give the students a sense of comraderie, a sense of belonging to a certain peer group; of living in a legitimate, respectable, and continuing tradition of literature written by local kids like themselves. The general emphasis is usually on imagery and events that occur where the students live and play, on familiar people and places. No matter what the poem is about, I ask the students that the feeling or idea be as real to themselves as possible. I am constantly looking for and trying to identify with their point of view. In this way, I feel that poetry will not only develop their language skills, but it will also develop the students' sensitivity and creativity. It is my belief that poetic self-understanding can help students develop to their fullest potential as human beings.

Assuming that all students have their own innate sense of rhythm in their speech, and that a few statements concerning imagery, simile, and symbolic language are more than enough to absorb in the average five day visit, much of the time in class is spent thinking and talking about content, subject, theme.

Assuming that it is appropriate, I try to follow the students' direction and interests—searching for the ones that seem to most illuminate them, that make them feel human as completely as possible.

Since the conventional models have often been more of an obstacle than an aid in sparking interest in literature, I usually rely on a selection of poems from other local students I've worked with, using their writings as models in both form and content.

A wide range of thoughts and feelings can be expressed by students, and once they realize that in their own way they fit in, it's not so difficult to get them to write freely. I try to make it clear that saying what they feel like saying as clearly as possible is the most important thing, and that spelling and grammar is secondary. The main thing is to first let their ideas flow, one after another. They should follow the guidelines and rules I set up, but if any rule becomes a problem while writing, they should break the rule, as long as it will help them in their writing.

When I go into the schools I sometimes see myself as a poetry salesman displaying an array of poems, looking for the ones that most students will identify with, ones that will inspire them to write their own. And when they write, I am on the lookout, not so much for polished writing, but for writing of substance.

This does not mean I am only looking for self-expression. I am looking for images and feelings a child projects in writing which make connections. I am looking for the relationships he or she makes with the world. I am looking for his or her view of the way things are, and hopefully, the way things can be, for the individual child and for the group. This kind of substance, this kind of beauty, is essential to art.

Treating student writing with an artistic attitude is, I believe, the best way to help the student approximate his or her potential for creating and appreciating poetry.

Chapter 1: Imagery

The brown waterfall   tastes   like chocolate   spit.

One of the first things I discuss in class is the importance of imagery in poetry. To do this, I ask the students to think about something which many find unpoetic at first.

I ask them to think about their bodies, their brains, and how we get to know things. Since everything we know comes through the physical senses, I ask them to think about the five senses: seeing, touching, hearing, smelling, and tasting.

It is said that the majority of imagery in poetry is visual imagery, but all the senses can be evoked using words. To convince them of this, that mere words can evoke physical feelings in a person just through listening, I ask the class to close their eyes and listen to a one-line poem written by Kelly at Hickam Elementary which I visited with poet Wayne Westlake. I ask them to think about which senses they are using as each word in the poem is spoken. I speak the words slowly:

The brown waterfall   tastes   like   chocolate spit.

When the moans and sounds of people licking their lips die down, we are ready to discuss the poem. The initial images evoked are visual because of the color of the waterfall. This in turn evokes thoughts of mud, loud cold storms, overflowing splashing smelly water, and finally, the feel and taste in the mouth of chocolate spit, a strongly tactile image which everyone can relate to.

Though it is obvious, I point out the power one word can have, the use of the word "spit" being a good example of the

11

importance of word choice. It is a good example of a strong ending to an otherwise unexciting line, just by the addition of the last word to an otherwise complete sentence. It is an example of what the language can do if you push it to the limits of its own structure. It is an example of how poetry, which most think of as unexciting, can actually create a physical sensation within a person just by listening to the words someone has arranged in a pattern.

Another poem I like to share with classes is one by Eustaquio "Pads" Padilla from Waimea High School:

Under the whisper of the waves,
The sharp, jealous reef lies with its mouth open.
It screams for the taste of my feet,
Under the whisper of the waves.

I had originally thought it was a good poem because it had a good rhythm, it was easy to memorize quickly, the first and last lines acting as a kind of refrain.

Also, the poem is focused on an oral motif. I read it to classes and ask them to count how many references it makes to mouths or something related to the mouth.

And the poem is easy to identify with for anyone who has spent time near the ocean, as most islanders have.

But what really clinched the poem was hearing Pads read it in class. We were taping everyone, using the speaker of the tape recorder to monitor the voices so everyone could hear it as it was being recorded. When it was his turn he gently squeezed the small microphone in his football player's hand, and looking down, he quietly recited the poem, from memory, in perfect Kauai pidgin.

Although the poem is written on the page in perfect English, it was an unforgettable experience to have the additional touch of the inflection and music of the speaker's voice. This kind of genuineness in poetry is something we look for when we read or listen to a poet. A true voice is something which has always persuaded an audience to believe that what a person is saying is authentic or sincere. The kind of aural imprint this poem makes in the mind is another kind of imagery. It is something hard to perceive on the written page, but from the time I present this example to classes, everyone becomes more aware of what a poem sounds like when read out loud. And students also become conscious of the possibilities of using pidgin, which many still speak as their first language.

A few poems follow to further illustrate the importance and effectiveness of imagistic writing.

Some have to do with personal feelings, or observations of other people.

Others are taken from nature, sometimes making comparisons to the artificial world, a timeless job of poets everywhere, no matter what age.

Some move beyond depictions of the so-called "real world." With one foot remaining in reality, Sidney at Pauoa School convinces you:

The boy kissed the slug till its
pimple turned to ice.

Or Lori Taketa from Maemae School gets you to envision:

A herd of wild marbles is rolling
down New York City

13

Or employing a technique called *synaesthesia*, a kind of mixing of the senses, Darlene at Kauluwela School shows you a new definition of "loud colors":

The bunches of flowers had brightened me with their noise

It's so clear you believe it too. The creativity and clarity with language begins to move toward poetry where just one image, one mental picture or sensation, triggers an identification within the reader which becomes an experience in itself. All the reader must do is take the time, even for a short poem, to absorb the image, to let it grow into whatever shape it takes in the mind.

I like to compare the short image poem to a bud. There is so much color and fragrance waiting to be discovered. Or, as Lance Lewis from Nanakuli High says:

How quick the mind bloom when it knows a secret!

Wouldn't it be nice if there was nothing
but space between your ears
with a couple stars shining?

Wade Kyono
Kalani High

My eyebrows are like chicken feathers when I wake up.

Ernest
Koloa Elementary

This morning I look in my mirror
and my eyes look like
two pheasant's eggs.

Kamaunu
Lanai Elementary

A crab scurried like a gathering of ashes

Calvin
Pearlridge Elementary

The rocks were big
but the water ate them off into mud

Liane Miyamura
Maemae Elementary

When the eel bit my brother
it was like a sunrise in the water

David K.
Iroquois Pt. Elementary

When a cricket sings
it's like making rock into ash.

James
Iroquois Pt. Elementary

Chewed bubble gum looks like the inside of a snail.

Leslie
Pearlridge Elementary

The green frog kisses as fast as I can turn my body.

Cindy Kubota
Pearlridge Elementary

She had a belly dancing attack in the mud.

Michelle
Ahuimanu Elementary

soft feet   silver feet

Maggie
Kauluwela Elementary

I can run faster than my father's tears can come out.

Michael
Pauoa Elementary

Fathers
are
the strongest
hill at the
end of the
road

John Maria
Kauluwela Elementary

Every day our parents drive cars
But what happens if they drive us?

Kent
Lanai Elementary

My father sleeps like an earthquake
when he's drunk.

Sheldon
Koloa Elementary

There is a crumbling small hill in my grandmother.

Patricia
Pearlridge Elementary

An old mountain erupts with pleasure
under the fingers of my grandfather.

April Moa
Nanakuli High

your daughter is too
        curved which she is
        afraid of

Carverlynn Manini
Roosevelt High

Crawl as small as you can get.

Maile
Pearlridge Elementary

Sometimes I have problems like a turtle curled up.

Laurie Ing
Pearlridge Elementary

Tangled Fingers

Tangled fingers
   white and wet
   sitting in a lap
   in a room full
   of strangers

Reynette Au
Kalani High

When we play baseball
and it starts to rain
I feel like eating the cloud.

Edgar
Lanai Elementary

People fighting in war
Ants dueling for a speck of food

Earl
Kalani High

The man is sitting on a chair
and is eating with a spoon
he is eating a pie and sits by
the window his eyebrow is big

Nadine
Kaunakakai Elementary

Slow Pin

Everything's
in slow
motion, bodies
entangled,
legs, arms,
one overpowering
the other.
Then the move,
slowly,
slowly the
pin and a
sharple whistle
and the
sound of a
slap on the mat.

Tricia Kaneko
Kalani High

Rocks
are
hard
like
boards
have
splinters
in
them
could
hurt
you
like
a
bee
buzz
when
I
see
it
fly
away
like
a
bird
when
you
scare
it
from
its
nest
has
straw
that
they
take
from
the
barn
is
red
painted
by
men
that
are
tall
like
a
giraffe
is
spotted

Tracey M.
Mililani Waena Elementary

40

A Piece of the Moon

I can feel a cold light
near the jewelry store,
I can feel something gleaming
as if a piece of the moon.

Victor
Pearlridge Elementary

Like a hot cup of cocoa
is what my tub of bathwater
feels like.
My body feels like a
mass of chocolate doughnut
as I slide into my warm,
inviting tub of water.

Donna Dong
Kalakaua Intermediate

The Glass Teacher

When she thinks
it's like you can see
through her.
Looking for the
correct answers.
Giving right answers.
Seeing through to
her mind. Glass
teacher. It's like
you can see right
through her.

Julia A.
Wilson Elementary

Chapter 2: The Family

I love everybody
especially my mother
and father
they look at me
with a smile
on their faces
and touch my soft skin
as if they were
touching themselves

Anonymous

One of my favorite themes is a discussion of family. Not
only is it a universal theme, making it an easy writing
exercise and genuine in feeling; but it is also an important
subject to children who are constantly making adjustments
within the family as they are growing up.

Since families provide a sense of continuity and belonging, and because a child's cultural background is learned within the family, this subject is also a good illustration of how literature is born out of and representative of a given culture. I want them to realize that what they are writing is not only a personal expression of their lives, but that it is also revealing of how people in this place and time behave.

When we discuss poems about various relatives, one of the things we do is make a list of all the possible relatives to write about. I ask for terms in different languages too, and ask that they use them if that is the normal way of addressing a relative. Once this discussion is over, the theme of writing about family naturally emerges from time to time during successive writing exercises.

One of the main issues that arises out of this theme is the question of harmony within the family unit. The poem at the beginning of this chapter expresses a basis for family unity in an image that is at once real and symbolic.

At the same time, more and more children come from single parent homes. The first poem on the subject, written by an anonymous 5th grader at Waipahu Elementary which I visited with poet Caroline Garrett, surprised me. But since then, I have discussed divorce with classes and found that many students know the experience and seem to be more accepting of it than I thought they would be.

In my body
there are caves
leading to different places.
I see blood and nothing but blood and dark.
Sometimes I see bones.
And veins and meat.
I am scared to be in the dark
so I think of my dog Pierre who died of
        heartbroken.
He's a poodle and is not supposed to be
        alone.
I let him go and he walked out of the gate.
Usually he runs.
I cried and cried
and I cannot forget about him.
My best dog I ever had for a long time.
Now I only have my cat Timothy
who is still a kitten that would want to mate.
And that's why I feel so lonely inside
of my great big body.
Nobody to love and care for.
Nothing but dark and death.
Sometimes I miss my father who left me
in Kindergarten. I visit him in summer.
He has his own family.
Now I am nothing to him.
But a body of dark and blood.
I live with my mother
who cares for me.
What else can anybody expect.

And this poem is in a similar vein. It also echoes the theme of the physical features of a family being one aspect of oneness.

My mother lives in Las Vegas my father
lives in Hawaii. I am my father's son
and my sister is icky. Our family has
small noses and soft faces. If you
ask me one day I will soar like an
eagle to visit my mother.

Mark
Makaha Elementary

Another aspect of tension within the family is the inevitable
sibling rivalry. The two poems which follow illustrate some of
the effects of such squabbling. The first one introduces the
use of the racial slur in name-calling. It astounds me that this
epithet could be used within the same family.

She sits there and don't do
nothing and when I tease her
she just sits there
but when I finish saying
Stupid Dumb Haole
my sister gets mad and then
she hits me, and I
run away and I tell my
mother and my sister
gets me later.

Kuulei
Lincoln Elementary

the lonely one

my brother
is always standing
by himself
it all started
from my sister
and her friends
she did not let him
play with them
so that is why
he is always
alone.

William
Lincoln Elementary

But there are also examples which demonstrate the urge to keep the family together. The following two poems display this emotion, one a physical and one a verbal hanging on.

Soft Hands

When I touch
my Aunty's
hand, it is so
soft, that I
will not let
go because
it's too soft
to let go.

Ann
Palisades Elementary

I like to swim with my grandfather in the cave
and the slow soft water tingles my spine
and all my problems leave me. It's like magic.
I like to listen to my grandfather's stories,
he talks so slow and he doesn't leave anything out.
Grandmother has three syllables.

Karen H.
Kaelepulu Elementary

In the poem "Snow Horses" by Ronald G. of Solomon Elementary, there is a strong sense of brothers sharing their dreams. Also, it is one of the few poems written in Hawaii which utilizes the image of snow in a believable way.

Snow Horses

My brother and I are snow horses.
Wanting to plow through great snow fields.
Our dreams have almost vanished.
But being snow horses
we can wait.

In "The Universal Noise" by Owen of Solomon Elementary
we are shown the difference a few years can make in his
attitude toward his sister.

The Universal Noise

The universal noise is talk
or the sound of feet
when you walk
My sister is always talking
and walking
teeth chopping

She's older now
and doesn't talk
quite as much
her feet have a
lighter touch
now she walks and talks
with much more poise
and *that's* the
universal noise

Another kind of writing about family that often occurs is the eulogy, a poem written in praise of someone. Poems about older relatives, grandparents, are often in this vein.

Baban, My Greatgrandma

My great grandma's skin
is wrinkled very much.
Like when you stay in the water
for a great long time.
When you get out of the water
it clears up. But I know that
hers will never fade.
Sometimes she calls me in her
room, she says pretty soon Baban
die. I feel sad and I'm silent.
She is so brave. She is the
great sweet apple waiting to be
eaten.

*Jason
Kalakaua Intermediate*

Soft Earlobes

My grandfather
has very soft earlobes.
As I massage his back
I flick his earlobe
and it wiggles back and
forth. It is soft
probably because I kept
pulling it when I was
a baby and it came loose
and soft.

Alex Shimizu
Wilson Elementary

There are also many elegies written, lamenting the loss of a loved one. Here is one exmaple by Manolo Delos Reyes from Waimea High.

a feather dropped
while I was taking a walk at night
I was remembering my old, short
grandmother who is dead now
now that she is gone, there is
silence like the loose sand in the
desert with no wind or no one

Following are a few more examples of poems about family. They all show a different kind of respect for relatives, moving toward understanding and sympathy for their points of view.

Clear Eyes

Clear Eyes, Clear Eyes
When I slammed the cardoor
on my dad's thumb
he didn't cry, he kept
clear eyes, and when he
made a fist and hit the
top of the car and made
a dent in it
he had clear eyes
clear eyes

Tamatha F
Solomon Elementary

Blue Hand

My mother always
opens her hand
in her hand I see
her love for me.

When she opens her hand
it turns to blue.
She touches my face
I feel she gave me her love.

My mother hugs me
her hand turns blue.
She takes my hand and
I take hers.
That's how we know
we love each other.

Helen Longao
Royal Elementary

When the man comes home he takes off his hat
combs his hair and looks out the window
through the trees at the sea

James
Kaunakakai Elementary

The spiders web is soft like
my mother's hand
which is noiseless when she moves it.

Michele Kemble
Lincoln Elementary

Don't Shoot

Yes his name is Yong Kuk
oh no everybody is teasing him
no   stop that   don't shoot
          the gun
don't kill him
under the car
don't kill my father just because
he has a funny name

Yu-kyong
Kaahumanu Elementary

Wrinkled Face

Wrinkled face
my grandma has
a wrinkled face
she has a wrinkled face
but a beautiful one
she does things for us
everytime she does something
it gets more wrinkled
but beautiful
wrinkled face

Faith Joy Woo
Pearlridge Elementary

God's Hug

God's Hug is when
My Tutu walks
She walks very slow
It makes me think
God's hugging her

Kaipo
Royal Elementary

My sister has shiny soft hair
and it is the color when the sunset
and all the boys like to dance with her
so she expects to cry so she bites
her fingernails

Linda
Pauoa Elementary

64

My brother's body is like
a dark room
with soft pillows

Gina Manzano
Pauoa Elementary

Chapter 3: Getting The Belt

I have noticed over the years that punishment is a crucial issue for children, because it arises from time to time in their writing. Perhaps the first example which stood out was by Claude at Maili Elementary.

I fell into the mud and my skin got muddy
my father grinned at me
he was slowly getting the belt
with his hand he twist my ears

What struck me initially was an identification with my own childhood, and fearing the belt or twist of the ears from my parents or older relatives. It seemed to be an accepted way of punishment at the time. And whether or not the child deserved punishment in the given situation, it seems important that he can talk about it, share it, and as in most cases, laugh about it with the class. They all understand. It is a theme they can all relate to. A kind of unity is reached which all can share, and they are healed in knowing this, that they are not alone in this painful situation.

Children are aware of their parents' attitudes towards lessons and punishments. They often make observations as to whether or not their parent is grinning or swearing or trying to be calm. They do try to make value judgments as to the validity of the lesson and the method of learning. And sometimes it is hard to deny their point of view.

Claude's poem raises the theme of care for ones body and material possessions. As we can see by the following poem, this is not only a matter of skill and physical coordination, but also a matter of attitude.

Joni is like a dog
Never get to play indoors
for I always have to play
outside
in our yard by myself
If I play inside my mother
scolds me cause I might break
valuable things
*but there's nothing valuable
in our house anyway!*

Joni
Koloa Elementary

And how many of us haven't had the urge to draw or write on a wall or piece of furniture at home or in public places. In this poem by an anonymous Koloa student, I can sympathize with child and parent in what seems to be a universal problem.

Bigdaddy

bigdaddy bigdaddy
slap me in da head
cause I had draw on the wall
I run out da house and he
chase me with a knife
when he catch me he pull my
hair bigdaddy bigdaddy
why you act mean
as one bear?

As for taking care of one's body, the following poem demonstrates a loving way to be taught a lesson. Because the lesson is presented so gently, many students need to hear the poem twice before they understand that it is concerned with an attitude about strength.

Fall to the Floor

When I was 1 years old I fell
to the floor in the house.
I had tears in my eyes but I
didn't cry out loud. So my
mommy and daddy hugged me and
hugged me and taught me a
lesson.

Ricky
Lanai Elementary

One of the main sources of conflict arises when a child mistreats his siblings or friends. As in many other situations, children usually know when they are doing something wrong but they do it anyway. Perhaps this explains why they will just stand there and accept their punishment when it does happen, and why sometimes they will even go and get the stick which is to be used on them. I always ask them why they do that, why they don't verbally object or even run away, and they just laugh and say that it would only make the punishment worse.

Bad Boy

One day when I was ten years old
I had a punishment because I
punched my brother's nose.
It was in the room and
no one was around us.
My parents had said
be good to my brother
and the lesson I had was belted
all around my body
and it was bad.

Lester
Lanai Elementary

The Big Bite

When I was around 4 or 5 there was this boy named Sonny.
We was playing, going play house. He was going be the
mother and so we went my house. We had a bag full of play
clothes. He put some on and I called him fagget so he
punched me. Now I was so mad I bit him in the face. Was
bleeding so I had run. My sister saw so she told my father
and he was looking for me so I crawed inthe bushes and I
was scared so then I got out of the bushes and when I
turned around there he was. He gave me lickens and from
this day on I never will bite a boy.

Michelle Pittsinger
Lanai Elementary

One sensitive subject concerning bodies is the children's knowledge of sex. Most of them seem to have a sense of shame which makes them giggle when they hear the following anonymous poem.

I can't say it because
if my mom finds out she will
kill me and I do mean kill me
because it has a bad explanation
I can't say what it is because
my mom will kill me if she knows
that I have seen it or that I
know what it looks like
the soft body

The term "hard head" has come up a few times, referring to a stubbornness beyond common sense. In the poem below by Shawn there is a mixture of admiration and rejection about his father's attitude towards work. By a show of hands in class, most of the other students said they would not likely emulate Shawn's father.

Hard Head

My father is really hard head sometimes.
He go work mostly every weekend and
when he sick he still like go work.
His boss tell him take vacation but
he no like he one real hard head bugga
man I tell you he really must love
his work boy I tell you he one real
hard head bugga.

Shawn
Koloa Elementary

In the poem by Greg, a 4th grader from Lanai School, the use of the term for the son is being turned around and applied to the father. Again, for the adult reader, the adjustment to a small 7 year old's point of view must be understood to understand the poem.

When I was 7 years old
I was outside by our yard
and my father tells me to
get the tool box and I say
to my father, It is too heavy,
and my father says to me,
you hard head.
He gets the toolbox
and I say to myself,
Why does he call me hard head?

Another common theme in the discussion of lessons and punishment is the child's feeling of wanting to retaliate, either for a punishment given, or for some unrelated incident, like not being allowed to go to the store. Children will sometimes go to extremes to get back at their parents for what they perceive as an injustice, and sometimes parents don't know until later what is taking place. Children are always testing to see how far they can go without incurring more punishment, but it usually doesn't take them long to find out what the limits are.

When I was 8 Years Old

When I was 8 years old
I came home later for supper.
My mom said for my punishment
I was grounded for 1 week.
I felt like slapping her face.
But then I knew
she was doing it for my own good.
After a few minutes I forgot
about being grounded for my own
good and I kept on snobbing her
for the rest of the week.

Grace Barnacha
Lanai Elementary

When I was 5
I got locked in my room
and never ate lunch.
When my sisters came
in the room
I swore to them.
I learned my lesson
to not play with matches
so my mom said
If you ever do that again
you will have to stay
a week in your room.
And after my mom go away
I make faces to her
and she don't know.

Ronald
Lanai Elementary

My mom went to the store.
She didn't let me go and I was really mad.
I went outside. I looked at that nice bunch of flowers.
I found a stick and I wacked it and I went in the house
and I watched tv.
Then my momma came home and looked at that big mess I made
and my mom said, "Who did this?!" and my mom looked at me.
She took the stick and told me, "Jenny, come out of there!"
and I said "no" and she said "Come now!" and I did
and she wacked me. Then I cried.

Jenny Figuerres
Lanai Elementary

One of the most startling stories of a confrontation with a
parent came from a sincere, quiet third grader who actually
read the poem out loud and brought howls from the class.
There is a lot to be learned about the shock value of words,
and once this is aired, the class can move on with some
sense of maturity about themselves. Again, just the sharing of
the experience—something which they all thought of doing
but had never actually done—is a way for them to get a
perspective on themselves, as well as their peers.

The Bad Word

When I was
four my mother
was cooking
dinner and I was
standing by the
stove in the
kitchen. My
mom said to
go away or I
might get burned
but instead I
said fuck you to my
mom. So my
mother got a
hand paddle
and spanked
me hard and
I started to
cry, so I ran
away from
there and I
never went near
that place for a
day.

Anonymous

I should explain that whenever I bring up this lesson on lessons and punishment, I try to make it as comfortable and humorous as possible. I don't want anyone to feel inhibited or ashamed about the matter, so I try to establish right away that it is a universal experience.

When I ask them by show of hands how many of them have ever been punished by their parents, the response is unanimous. When I ask how many have ever been hit by their parents, the response is at least 99% of the class. We discuss the various methods of punishment: scolding, swearing, no food, no television, being grounded, or being spanked with hands, belts, slippers, or various kinds of sticks.

I always ask them to think about the lessons they were supposed to be learning by these punishments, and whether or not they think it is fair, deserved or not. I always ask them to think about whether or not they will be like their parents when they grow up, or if they will modify their methods of coping with children. They seem to understand that they are going through an unavoidable but painful phase, and they expect the tension to lessen as they become adults.

One of the more frightening observations made by a student touches on the distinction between punishment being applied as a lesson of some kind, and unreasonable abuse. Hopefully, the sharing of such experiences will lead to a better understanding of the problem when it does occur.

I am a doll being murdered by a kid.
he does this because his mother
is doing it to him.
I can't do nothing about it
but I hope he'll be alright.

Anonymous

Chapter 4:
Friends, The Sparkle Like The Diamonds

I am the eyeball looking at you
But when you look at me I turn around
But oh, when we look at each other
My eyeballs turn from brown to blue
like yours
And when you look me straight in the eye
You see the sparkle like the diamonds.
My eyes are the key to you.

Kaipo
Royal Elementary

Related to the theme of family is the theme of friendship. Just as children must make adjustments within their families, they must also cope with relationships among their peers, at school and in their neighborhoods.

The process of making friends is an awkward one for many children. In Kaipo's poem above, the initial hesitancy and the final harmony are both present, bringing the blue and brown eyes into the clear light of a diamond.

81

However, children are also aware of many examples of false friendship. In cases such as these, they like to think of ways to get revenge, as in the following poems.

Marcia is like a piece
of Kleenex sometimes.
Sometimes some of her
so-called friends pick her
out of the box to blow
their noses.
And when they don't need her
anymore they throw her away.

Sometimes, after they blow
their noses with her, for revenge
the wind helps her and she likes to
go up to their faces to smother
and kill them.

Marcia
Wilson Elementary

Blake is like a baseball
being thrown down the plate to be hit
these men that are batters
they are my unkind brothers
so are the fielders
that I hate
oh so much
they hit me to short stop and
throw me to home
I feel like beaning them
in the batters box and when they
hit me I get all dirty on my seams
I roll inside their glove and roll
into their face.

Blake Oshiro
Momilani Elementary

83

At other times, frustrations surface, sometimes only to be expressed in a poem:

I feel like making a flower
with someone's face.

Emerle Guillen
Lanai Elementary

Or sometimes, fights will occur, such as the one recounted by Jeffrey Badua of Kalakaua Intermediate.

When I was five I wen start grade school at Kalihi-Kai.

I was playing outside by the jungle gym, planny kids was playing.

I wen block the way for go out of the jungle gym. Then this boy Joel wen say, "Eh watch out, I like go out!" But I neva listen to him. Then he wen push me from the back. I got up, turned around, faced him, and he wen punch my stomach. I was croakin on the ground. Den I got up, picked up some dirt and wen shovem up his face. Afta dat he wen grab my hair and we wen start scrappin. He started to cry because I tink I wen punch his head one hard one. He wen run and tell Ms. Sugihara the teacher. She came up to me and said, "Come here."

I said, "For what?!"

Den she wen grab my arm and put me in the classroom corner. She said to me, "You are not going to talk or move from this corner or I'm going to bring you to the principal's office."

I wen stay ova there the whole day. But after school she let me go home but she told me, "Never fight again or else I am going to have to call your parents, ok?"

I told her, "Ok!"

From then on I learn neva fight in da school. Bring da guy home and den beatem up.

One of the emotions which often accompanies friendship is the feeling of longing for someone. In February, Beth Hammer at Mililani Waena Elementary gave me a red, cut-out heart, on which she had written:

You eat my heart out Valentine

And Angela at Kaelepulu Elementary developed this
imaginary scene of waiting for a friend who may never come.

1
I wait in the valley for the sunset
and you. To come and see the
beautiful deer as they drink
from the spring.

2
The water fall goes up
because someone is pulling
and pulling and won't let go

3
I wait and wait on the beach
for you to come. The sun sets
and you are not here. Hurry
before the great eagle takes me
over the golden mountains.

Sometimes even friends will tease, picking on some peculiarity or idiosyncracy of a person, and that can be enough to bring a child to tears.

Crybaby   when somebody teases
Cries softly without tears
Sitting quietly body moving up and down
Scared to let anyone know he is hurt

Harvey
Kaahumanu Elementary

Sometimes children tease by making up nicknames for someone. When I bring up this subject in class, everyone seems to have their own favorite nicknames for people. We talk about whether or not the person deserves the nickname, if it is appropriate, and whether or not they think that the person will be hurt by other people talking about him this way. When they write poems about peoples' nicknames, I ask them to be precise, but to try to be gentle or funny so no one will be hurt. Here are two examples.

His nickname is roadrunner.
The first time I saw him
do it was when we played
kickball. He runs with his
arms on the side flapping
his hands back and forth
and his legs in back of him
running, and his head in
front making his mouth like
he's kissing someone

Eric Nagata
Kaahumanu Elementary

Chicken Wings

She lives next door
She's not a friend
She's kind of fat
Sometimes she's cocky
(meaning weird)
She always flaps her
wings back
She does it because
she likes to stick out
her chest
She thinks she has
a big chest
She does it on purpose

Lynda
Kaahumanu Elementary

Chapter 5: Romance

A Bite of Love

When I'm in love
So very much
I take a bite out of
A heart.

Lianne Mahoe
Royal School

Related to the theme of friendship is love. Romance is a
popular subject, especially among the secondary level
students, and the hardest part in utilizing this theme is to avoid
poems which are too sentimental, trite or mushy. Also, many
of the love poems which are strongly written are also nega-
tive in tone. Failed or fantasized love relationships are
common.

91

Nevertheless, love poems are unceasing in their energy, as exemplified in this short one by Roberta of Konawaena High.

Love can make you go over a waterfall.
The lake in my eye is meant for you!!

In the following section we are given a glimpse of the anxiety, heartbreak, and the humor of romance among local teenagers and pre-teens.

First Time

Feeling good
No worries
Holding his hand
Not thinking
Of my sweaty palm

Kris Miyasato
Kalani High

Taking the time
to wash my hair,
put on nice clothes,
and make up my face.
Only to what?
Go out to sit in a car
and cruise with someone
who I've known for years?

Yvonne Lee
Kalani High

I am a woman who sits in my
room. I paint darkness and terror,
my life has been surrounded
by gravestones.

My man appears at night.
My hair is gold.
By day it is black.

Kimi Baker
Konawaena High

Romance!
dirt was what you did
beautiful is what I am
calculator is like how I work
piece paper is our marriage license
sun is heat when you're mad
sit in my desk and think of you
like a cotton you're smashing in my
face

Sharon B.
Nanakuli High

The three stars sparkled in the midnight sky
as he gently kissed her
feeling the warmth of her body

her eyes were like ice
engaged in the thoughts from the mirrors of her mind
as she stared out at the racing ocean of gray

Jo Ann Hirata
Roosevelt High

The flames of
her lips that begin to dry
skinny cracks that begin to form.
Big lies that lie within them,
and the cold sorrow of her tongue.

Jason Ebalaroza
Nanakuli High

The clouds covered the sun like the darkness
of hate covered my heart
As the darkness grew into my heart
it destroyed my feelings of love
which turn to the dark color of red
red like blood which bursts out through
my hands as I stroke him with
the knife.

Nora
Konawaena High

Three Foxy Chicks walking on air to the Bus Stop
I stare with my November Brown slippery eyes
One wore a rice white kimono while sucking on a
    blue salt soft spiny lollipop
the other a face like a black rose, her body like
    a slippery eel
The third had a pot belly, but a face like a
    glass swan...

Anonymous
Hickam Elementary

Dating girls
Am I gonna like it
Not on Blind Date Radio
You knucklehead

Do What?
Ask what she like
Wear. Go
To a boring movie?
Eat what?
Pizza?

Danny Dartez
Royal Elementary

Uno da odda night ha
me and my friend
wen go see one bad movi you know
and was real bad you know
but everybody like dat kine movi
cuz they bad das why
I wanted to leave da teata
but my friend said we go stay
I said why and she said cuz
she need experience

leslie n.
Nanakuli High

we was goin' try make ah!
but then we neva try
because we was too scared
so we neva make

Erwin
Kalakaua Intermediate

Chapter 6: Reaching Out

Some years ago, well-meaning people had laws passed which disallowed the promotion of specific religions in the public schools. Fortunately, poetry and all art forms are still taught and practiced and are perfect for keeping students in touch with that metaphysical, spiritual aspect of themselves.

Teachers can be useful guides in this process, but their primary concern, especially at the younger ages, is to create the feeling within each student that his or her thoughts and feelings are worth expressing, that each person has a soul which must be allowed to grow. Poetry, and all the arts, is an important part of that growth in all people.

The following selection of poems shows students reaching out in ways not normally given much attention in school. Starting with the idea of sleeping or dreaming as an entry into another world, they sometimes wander into a realm of spirits which includes ghosts of relatives or complete strangers. The examples presented here are sincere, first-hand accounts culled from half-forgotten, second-hand, faked, or made-up ghost stories.

Another kind of reaching out is when they begin to think about "God" and the meaning of existence beyond themselves. It is refreshing to see children thinking of the people in the world as sharing a common existence. And it excites me that some are developing a worldview which telescopes into the universe.

I close my eyes and let my brain wander,
but later I try to catch up with it
before it goes too far away where I can
never get it back.

Charlotte
Pauoa Elementary

When I wake up in the morning
I feel like a melted popsicle, refrozen.

Reiko
Koloa Elementary

Dream Eel

When you sleep
the dream eel
comes into your
melted mind
at the edge
of the world
so one side
of your house
will tip over
and you will
fall into the
edge of the
world.

Mung Ling Choy
Royal Elementary

When I try to go to sleep
I feel like a boat drifting
down a river to the reservoir
where I go to sleep
at the other end
of the reservoir

Joby!
Koloa Elementary

I was in bed asleep
when all of a sudden
I heard someone trying to get in.
I froze. I couldn't move or yell.
    Then I saw
        a white hand
        coming from the
        ceiling.
It came and touched my forehead
and I could move again.
It had lasted five minutes.
My mom said it was god.

Terri
Makalapa Elementary

Although my Grandfather has passed away his spirit still remains. To me he led a very interesting life. Selling shoes isn't very much, but what made it interesting is when I once told my friends that he was the one that made the glass slippers for Cinderella and not her fairy Godmother! I don't know why but I have this feeling that one day he will come back and live with us once more. My grandmother says that we can still communicate with him. I asked her how and she said, "By praying Bonnie, by praying." Ever since then I have been talking with him every night. I told him that we were going to leave Makaha Valley to live in Waianae and I asked if he would have to stay in the same place but he said, "No, wherever you go, I go!" and that made me rejoice every year.

Bonnie Ilaban
Makaha Elementary

One night when I was very young
I saw a ghost. I was in my own
bedroom in Kekaha, in bed, awake.
I was alone, no sisters, no brothers,
and my parents were asleep. Then I
looked into the doorway, and I saw
a ghost. He was dressed in a long
brown suit, over his feet, and
touching the ground, the sleeves
over his hands, a brown hood over
his head. When I looked at its face
I couldn't see anything, so his face
was black. He started to float
into my room, coming to my bed.
I screamed but my voice was gone.
I closed my eyes for a moment
and when I opened my eyes,
the ghost was gone.

Eric
Koloa Elementary

111

When I was 3 I saw a ghost.
It happened in my mother's
bedroom in Virginia. I was
ready to go to sleep.
The time was about 7:00.
It looked like my
granpa but only one thing
was different, the figure
had horns. And the figure
said Go Away.

Isaac
Koloa Elementary

I was small about six years old.
I was riding on a canefield road.
Looking around. When I was going
back home I saw a graveyard.
I was curious so I looked around.
Then I saw a man-like figure
walking around.
When I saw it I screamed.
When I was going home on
my bike I bumped into
something and nothing
was there.

Vance
Koloa Elementary

While sitting in church
the sun came flashing
through, and the closeness
of the people seems to
spread throughout my body

Emmylou Martin
Waimea High

One day I found some good seed...
I planted it and it became like a jewel
that shines between the branches
of the fires of life. I took a breath
and looked inside. It was like a chant
with no song, but it was the fire kindled
in me. But little did I realize that
the seed I planted would grow into a
great flame that will spread its fire branches
clutching out to lost souls and kindling
their life fires setting them ablaze
and in turn they light someone else's
life essence and we would become
like an endless wood...

Darlene Rita
Waimea High

The Happy Children

I would
feel very
sad for the
children. So
I would
give them
something
to eat because
they look
hungry, and
sad.
When I
give them
food they
start to
feel happy.
Then I
start to
feel happy.
There's a
long line
waiting for food.
The lines comes
from tents
that are just
a little way
from here.
I don't care if
there's a long line
or not, I just want
them to feel
happy inside.

Jennifer Chow
Royal Elementary

116

Tomorrow, what will it bring?
Will it bring sadness or happiness.
Sometimes I wonder if tomorrow will
be the end of all life and then what
will happen, will everyone go to an
unknown world, will the evil or goodness
come out of us, or when we die will it
be a better place than we live in now.

Or will we just be in the air in which we
lived in, sometimes I wonder what
tomorrow will bring. And when all of us
die do you wonder if the birds will sing
and if the wind will blow or if the sun
will shine. Or how do you know if when
we die the ocean will drain. Or the
mountains will sink. I wonder what
tomorrow will bring.

Tracy
Kaelepulu Elementary

When I went outside
I saw the world turning
and it giggled around

Trisha Correia
Maili Elementary

When the sun set
the moon came up
and the stars fell
upon my eyes
while the Apollo 949
was on the moon
the martians hopped
star to star
like the stones
in the stream

Christine
Scott Elementary

planets scattered around like a game of marbles

Galen Komatsu
Palisades Elementary

I will dig an opening
in glass clouds in space
and crawl through them.
And I will find a hole in the deep
and I will crawl down it
and find myself here.

Peter Greenman
Kaelepulu Elementary

Chapter 7: Who Am I?

Whenever I visit a class I always tell them, "The main thing to remember is that every one of you has something inside you, a soul, and you all have something important to say—a true expression of that soul. There are lots of different things each person has to say, and it's up to you to decide what's important for you to say. No one else can tell you what's right for you to say. Only yourself. You have to listen to the voice inside you, in your mind and in your heart, and let your thoughts and feelings be guided by your faith, your belief.

You can be guided by other people, too. You can get clues for your own feelings and your own life, by seeing what other people have to say from their point of view. When I read poems by other people, you should listen and see if you can understand what they are trying to communicate.

But in the end, you must trust yourself.

Learn to do this when you are young, and it will be easier for you to grow."

Whenever students write a poem I try to make some kind of response, either verbal or written. My initial reactions are sometimes technical or structural, and sometimes just feedback as to what I like or don't like, what I would like to see expanded or deleted. But I always try to respond with something positive, even if to comment that they have un-knowingly created a simile by using the world "like" in their poem; or to let them know that I identify with the point of view expressed in the poem; anything which I can honestly say is good in what they have put down on paper. This is necessary if any person is to feel that what they have done is worthwhile, worth continuing, for if there seems to be even a little room for growth in any given direction, the possibilities for expansion become infinite.

At Nanakuli High, one of the schools I visited with poet Jody Manabe, a girl named Lori-Ann wrote a poem which is a response to this kind of nurturing attitude. This is a basic attitude which we all must cultivate if we are to be successful, no matter what kind of teaching we do.

TO YOU FOLKS

You must be the type of person
who really enjoys and understands how
an ugly piece of something could
still look beautiful / try and
              imagine
                  that

I will share and share my shine!

Sherman
Lincoln Elementary

The flowers are blooming
The flowers smell good
the flowers are wild
And so are you.

Loraina
Lanai Elementary

I am
the
golden
reaction
against
the
sharp
colors.

Thuan Nguyen
Royal Elementary

Some people tries
to tell you how
you are like and
what you are like
just by looking at
you and seeing
someone like you
no matter how far
away they are

But to me I am
a person of feeling
of blue and beautiful
things that are colorful
by its own self

Clint
Waimea High

Heartbird

Heartbird is a
very strange word.
It means if you
pick up a bird
its heart beats
so fast because
it's nervous.
I have a
heartbird myself.

Dawn
Iroquois Pt. Elementary

No where is my name
Hard to keep and not easy to tame
Unlike others I have no road, no ends
No light load but heavy burdens
Going over the endless oceans

Jocelyn Vo
Kaahumanu Elementary

I am not a maze
I will not trap you
I will help you find your way

Paul Imai
Kalani High

I am calm as the seawind
Seawind always calms my soul
So anyone may come and talk with me
And the calmness will be passed on
as the seawind passed to me
Next time you go to the beach take a deep breath of seawind
and then pass it on.

Paul Imai
Kalani High

I like to wear soft clothes
that make me feel
I'm really sharp.

Anna Coyaso
Waimea High

I am a toothbrush facing every
morning a stink mouth. I have
nothing to look forward to,
always the same old things. I
am always being used to make
people feel happy, yet I, myself,
am full of sorrow for my dull
life. I am a toothbrush facing
everyday, a stink mouth.

Beatrice Martin
Royal Elementary

Nhung is like a
Hardly full
Universe
Not too many ships enter it
    for not even the bravest man dares to
Go through it

Jocelyn Vo
Kaahumanu Elementary

My hands are horses
galloping in the wind.
They pull my body
in the wind.
My hands are brown
and wet.
Making a loud sound.
They want to fly high.

Pamela Matsumoto
Royal Elementary

I listen to the beat of the music
I always pretend to be a drummer
or lead guitarist of a group
I like it always, even in my sleep
every night I listen to my radio
checking for the good songs
Sometimes I change the station for a better song
I listen to my radio like a tiger listens to its mother

Billy Kam
Kaahumanu Elementary

136

I am the president and people listen to me.
I live in a big white house because
I'm the president. I'm rich and I can buy
anything because I'm the president. I could
take a trip to other states then take another
and I could take my family with me because
I'm the president.

Preciosa B.
Nanaikapono Elementary

137

When I woke up this morning
I was a dog on the street
and nobody knew me
and they would just look at me
and walk away
so I got bored and
walked down the street
and looked for somebody I knew

Masamoto
Lincoln Elementary

Crying Shadow

Cry shadow   cry all you
want. Crying because
you lost your person.
Look in the alley
look in the street.
But don't cry shadow.
You don't need to.
You can do things
by yourself. Think
of what you can do.
So don't cry.

Won Han Cheng
Wilson Elementary

I know not where I come from
and know not where I am going.
The ringing of my thoughts
started when I was born
and will continue to ring forever
after I have gone from my body.

Christine
Nanakuli High

Chapter 8: Small Kid Time Hawaii

In the preceding sections, most of the poems were written conjunction with specific writing exercises or lesson plans, usually word association or imagery exercises. Sometimes the subject matter was the focus of class discussion, and in some cases, one writing exercise would lead to another, as in the case of family poems eventually spawning lessons and punishment poems.

In the following section, there are poems about humor, singing, death, war, feeling the blahs, animals, and nature. These subjects weren't assigned as lessons, but they could have easily become that.

Nature seems to be a major topic whenever children think of poetry, in addition to the fact that Hawaii instills a feeling for the environment which is unique. The other topics are the kind which crop up spontaneously in the poems students write, and if the class discussion focuses on any given subject, it could become the writing exercise for the day. All I'm trying to do, at times, is to institutionalize the local custom of talking story with the kids. If this process is successful, they will naturally have the urge to share their own experiences on the given subject of conversation.

Since I pass out dittoed copies of everyone's poems for analysis and appreciation, there is every chance for the class to finds its own direction. There are as many possible directions as there are students, and I am most comfortable when I feel the class is of one mind, sorting out ideas, and I am just along for the ride trying to keep everyone together.

This is an attitude I have been developing over the years, and I am just lately learning to be comfortable with it. After a recent visit to a school I wrote in my journal:

> You love to find a kid's mind coming to a thought.
> Open a few choice topics (on forms of punishment
> they're experts) and watch them find their own
> paths through all versions of experience thrown
> their way. Question those times their paths follow
> yours too closely. Tell them you can't lift your
> feet fast enough to avoid their growing stampede, and
> then you better run like hell!

Is your nose ready to sing?

Jeral Smith
Makaha Elementary

The mother said son go get a flea
The son said what kind sour or sweet

Leila
Nanaikapono Elementary

a slow moving bathroom
made a drunk
fall
into the drain

kelly
Makalapa Elementary

Nervous Fingers

When I am
shake when I
when I am nervous
when I am
shake.

Lynne Altieri
Pearlridge Elementary

The bumpy chicken

When I went to eat dinner
we were having chicken
I looked at the chicken
and it was covered with bumps.
When I looked at it
I started to get a tummy ache.
I could imagine eating it
with all the bumps coming off
in my mouth.

Stacey Yamamoto
Palisades Elementary

One day my daughter said to me,
she said so softly so quietly
Mommy I have a petunia in my ear,
that's why I can't hear you so clear.

Marilyn
Kaaawa Elementary

Sensitive Tunnels

Sensitive tunnels are
so sensitive that if
you put your fingers in it
your father complains

Sensitive tunnels are
sometimes dirty that you
have to clean it
frequently

Sensitive tunnels?

Alex Paauilo
Pearlridge Elementary

149

My grandmaddah always tell it
like it is to people.
One day she said
"You too short. Grow taller."
I said "How?"
She said "Stand up."

Margery Macadangdang
Kalakaua Intermediate

I have dimpled knees,
so I wish I could be a flea.

Lori
Pauoa Elementary

A Dark Music

Music is in everyones mind
But unless the song is sung
It remains dark music

Paul Imai
Kalani High

THE BLUE SKY SINGS TO ME EVERYDAY

Kristi Petelle
Kilauea Elementary

Don't look down your nose.
Even though you are rich
you can own a deer,
a place that circles the cliff,
and a white seed that needs the moon to grow.
You still can never get a beautiful voice
like some poor people have.

Jaime Asao
Maemae Elementary

Her voice
like a lady singing
in a tidal pool of flowers
My friend sits and charms
the opihis off the rocks
I stare in wonder
and I am charmed off
balance into the tidal
pool of flowers

Robert Komaki
Waimea High

koa
sister
climb
the
valley
and
the
sharp
branches
point
straight
at
her
and
she
sing
and
sing

James
Kaunakakai Elementary

156

Ocean Shine

When the sun
goes down behind
the sea
and the moon
comes up
and makes a
silver path upon
the ocean's surface.
When the stars
come out and
start their songs,
and silent music
from the starlight
fills your heart.
That's when
the ocean
shines.

Tracy G.
Palisades Elementary

A sea monster
ate the ocean
the ocean started
a tidal wave, the
tidal wave started a
whirlpool, the whirlpool
banged the seamonsters
mouth to get out
the seamonster held
his mouth as tight
as he can, but
the whirlpool
knocked out all
of his teeth,
the teeth
cracked open
and mermaids
began to swim out,
then the mermaids
began to sing.

Cevin Kihano
Ahuimanu Elementary

There was once an eel who would swim in the waves
who would expect a mynah bird to sing for him in the dark.
But instead the mynah bird would bark and the eel would
go crazy. "Ahhh," said the bird, "You must have cancer."
Blood ran down the eel's back. The eel said, "I don't
have much time to live and I am a loser I will never be
free like you. I always dream of a sexy redhead and I
have been waiting to see this Beauty. If she dies I
will cry and die and rise to a cloud and sway while I
travel the world and pray. And when I lookout of the
cloud for a moment I will look at Hana and I will cry
to make the morning dew."

Shelley Baker
Hickam Elementary

In the night
when the rain hits
the roof
I think I'm in one war
with the bombs dropping
when I'm in bed
ready to fight

Alex Dela Cruz
Lanai Elementary

Norberto is like an owl.
Short and has a big belly that's round.
Then it's over growing like a big round ball.
The army used him for a cannonball to hit Vietnam.

Norberto Garcia
Wilcox Elementary

Dry Blood

Dry Blood Dry Blood
What happens before
it's Dry Blood
Does it scream
for help in
the raging
hot sun or
does it sit
on its victim
and fade away
Dry Blood
Dry Blood
What happens before it's
Dry Blood

Jodi
Iroquois Pt. Elementary

I missed my uncles, aunties, and sisters because they are in the family. I could never get another uncle, auntie or sister. I sure missed them. I think they missed me too. Someday they'll come back. They were captured by da communist. I hate da communist. Everybody hates the communist and I'm one of them. My mother, grandma, and grandpa hate them too. Someday if I have the power I will take my revenge on them I swear to you I will. If I don't somebody will because da communist kine's got ta die.

Thuan
Royal Elementary

I'm an old story teller,
I tell them some stories
about old people. I tell
them not to be scared of
old people, I tell them
how they die, and to love
them, not to cry when they
die, I love children all
my life I love children,
so I tell them I will die
someday.

Kay Hamada
Waimea High

I watched my uncle
sadly laying in bed
and he said
in a calm whisper

now you won't need to worry
for I'll be like a cloud
just floating in the sky

Robert Takenouchi
Royal Elementary

I could feel the
brush of the
bird's flight
like the day my
mother died,
so calm, so quiet,
as if all living
creatures held
their breath until
the final moment
and then the rain
poured down as if
the heavens were all
crying for my
mother's death
and then it was
dead quiet...

Kathy Wheat
Waimea High

When life is getting to me
I wish I could crawl into a cave.
I'd like to scrape my skin
right off until you saw
the bone.

Walter K.
Nanakuli High

is my leg ready to bake
is my nose ready to bake
is my ear ready to kill
is my arm ready to cut
is my head ready to roast

Can you live if you go to hell?

Mark Fujii
Makaha Elementary

168

I went to work and it was boring.
I saw the boss and he was ugly.
I worked all day till I was finish.
Then I went home to sleep on my bed
with my gray blanket and brown pillow.

Randal Gersaba
Nanakuli High

Bones

Bones
My bones
clacking around
What holds them together?
How come a dog doesn't come
And take them away?

Tessie Zarsoza
Lanai Elementary

I Hate You

I hate you
You stupid scum
You talk to me
As if I were a dog
I hate you
You crazy, ridiculous
Mixed up bum
You throw me around
Like a rag doll
I hate you
For everything you do
I hate you
I hate you

Tessie
Lanai Elementary

The
door
moves
when
I
shoot
the
glass
and
it
breaks
all
over
the
clouds
in
the
sky

Paul
Scott Elementary

I was mad and I got a knife
But nobody was around
so I put it back

Jamie
Kaaawa Elementary

Red Brother

Red Brother
is my blood
brother that
I cut very
bad

Jeff
Wilson Elementary

Crazy Mongoose

There is a
mongoose who
lives in an
apartment
in the city
he drinks
all the time
day and
night. He invites
his friends over
to drink and
there is a big
racket in the
apartment
building.

In the apartment
in the city there
is a shelf with
whiskey bottles on it.
The room is
bare except for
the shelf and
bottles.

Pat Iwata
Momilani Elementary

Lonely Chair

Lonely chair
lonely chair
by the window
in my auntie's house
lonely chair
when no one sits
lonely chair, no one
has time to sit there
not even my auntie
lonely chair

Faith Joy Woo
Pearlridge Elementary

The Truth of the Grouchy Old Man
is remembering the loud voice
of the old man and the truth about
the old man as he yells and says
who left the toothpaste on the
ground and yelling about there's
no more after shave
but there is a truth in everything
even the grouchy old man

Jim McCann
Kaelepulu Elementary

a burning fireplace
crackling fire
an old man sitting in a large chair
fire getting smaller
the old man goes and gets fire wood
when the old man comes back
the fire is almost dead
he puts some wood in the fire
the fire gets very big again
it gets warmer and warmer
he is all alone
no one to talk to
no other houses around
his is very sad because his wife
died a few weeks ago
now he prepares his own meals
he only reads in his spare time
he has no dog or cat
it is very cold
he stares at the fire
as it gets bigger
the fire, it can do anything
the old man thought
I can almost do anything too
the old man thought again

Donna Kurisu
Kaelepulu Elementary

The wind is blowing. I disappeared into
a world that has beautiful flowers and fruits.

Deborah
Makaha Elementary

179

The breeze was cold
as I sat on the beach with a crab.
The grains were blowing in my hair.
Then a small snail crawled up.
And I was left sitting on the sand
with the animals.

Jennifer
Scott Elementary

I felt like a dog chasing rabbits in a pasture. I jumped to touch butterflies with my paws, and I ran around touching daisies and tiger lilies with my nose and smelling them. Then I ran and jumped on the rocks and looked at the world around me, and in a second I knew I wasn't alone.

Regina Silva
Lincoln Elementary

I is me. Me loves smooth waves. I thirst for waves. Growing and shining together and wandering with speed. I know my friends.

Tricia
Konawaena High

on the cool
        reef, fish
flow easy like the
        blood in my veins

Ricky Boyles
Waimea High

The
  wind
    is
      the
        sigh
          of
            the
              stars

Duane K.
Konawaena High

Morning comes.
Everyone is up.
I am still asleep.
Very quiet I wake up
in the shadow of a bird.

Melvin
Pauoa Elementary

My head is full of love
My hand likes to hold baby birds

Skip
Kilauea Elementary

I see you
an owl
see you owl
in a tree
you are hiding
in a tree
please come out
Please!

see me under a woods
I'm hiding for you

Lisa Befitel
Kaunakakai Elementary

Mynah,
sleep
in the
rain
inherit
spoiled illusions

Byron
Scott Elementary

Koa trees and trees I don't know surround my home blocking my view. Must find a sharp axe, cut down the trees I don't know, maybe I would cut down all of the Koa trees. I must have my view.

Yoshishige
Konawaena High

The Truth of the Volcano
can spirit out hot lava.
And let it run slowly
the side of the volcano
with sort of a crackling sound.
And destroy anything in its path.
When the pressure builds up
the volcano will erupt and the lava
will scatter like a cat ripping
the body of a mouse all up.

Brian Harrigan
Kaelepulu Elementary

Lava glowed over the rocks
it came from the mountain side
it came down to the Paakula family
they ran but it went over their house
they cried and cried so they went
to your house
they stayed over until they had a house

Noelani Kamakawiwoole
Makaha Elementary

Our World

Volcanoes
have
hot
lava
forms
into
island
green
trees
grass
park
near
water
smells
stink
like
rubbish
can
near
wall

on street
highway
cars
run
over
stink
rubbish
like
paper
cans
soiled
food
pollution
all
over
world
and
in
water
that's
blue
and
green
and
boats
on
water
sailing.

Henry R.
Scott Elementary

192

The blood
of a deer
was all over
the ground
because the
hunter used
his powerful
double barrel
rifle
to puncture
the deers
heart. The
deer struggled
to reach cover
but he
died before he
could. But
the sound from
the gun warned
the other
animals of
the hunter.
The blue
bird flew
away. The skunk
let out a bad
smell, and the
lion roared
because the
hunter shot
the deer.

Clay
Kaaawa Elementary

Climb upward
faster faster
The eel
The slipping eel
teeth shining as silver
My leg   My leg
You son of a bitch
My leg
Why not all of me

Thomas
Konawaena High

My friend
every time I
go fishing with
my friend he
tortures the
fish he catches.
He sticks his
fish under a
car tire and
the car squashes
it.

Derek
Lincoln Elementary

I am fishing and the water is still.
I feel that I am a lonely fish on land.
The air is still and nothing moves.
I lay down on the thick concrete wall and I close
my eyes and breathe the still air.
I hear the seagull and I fall asleep.

Adrian Liu
Royal Elementary

I saw my grandfather by the ducks
then I saw him trying to cluck

David
Makaha Elementary

When I go home I eat
then change my clothes
then go out and let my puppies
out and let them bite me.

Yvette
Lanai Elementary

Train

Train is what
you must do
if you want
your pet to
be good at
it.

Dan N.
Palisades Elementary

Cat's Eyes

Cat's
Eyes
glow
where
do
they
glow
not
in
the
sun
but
in
the
dark
why
do
they
glow
because
without
them
he
wouldn't
be
able
to
see.
When
cats
meet
each
other
cats
their
glows
glow
if
it's
a
girl
cat
the
glow
really
glows.
When
it's
a
boy
cat
the
glows
are
crossed
but
then
if
glows
cross
look
ut
out
and
get
away
from
the
fighting
cats.

Michelle Lindsey
Royal Elementary

200

soft feet

What makes a cat
have soft feet?

A rat!

Po Chun
Royal Elementary

I was thinking about
My horse Mongoose and what a stupid name it is.
We didn't name him the person that owned him before us did.
He said he named him that because he was riding him
from Kalae to Kamalo. Mongooses kept running
in front of him and he was trying to think of a
name. So he named him mongoose. Kind of stupid,
huh. I think he feels stupid about it. He thinks
he is so tuff but he's not. Every time he gets
his hoof stuck in his pasture fence he doesn't say
a word, just stands there.

Jackie West
Kaunakakai Elementary

The horses in the field
behind our school
with heavy hoofs you hear
them run by
but when you were here
the sounds went away
for it was an interesting subject
that subject of poems
poems of yours
poems of others
now and awhile you hear
those horses with heavy hoofs
so come back soon
before the horses in the field
behind our school

Edwin DeAguiar
Konawaena High

From The Front Of The Class

And you, silly fool,
do you realize
you're standing there
with your hands folded,
sneaking a prayer at them
every once in a while
begging for
I don't know whose sake
they'll write a poem
from the heart
of a good local kid
everyone would want
to claim as one
of their own?
Do you really think
they see the prayer
in your eyes
everytime you smile
into theirs, checking
to make sure
they got good
souls in there?
Is the gospel beginning
to come through?
All it needs now
is to be said
as clear
as a clear Hawaiian
day can be.
And then, I think,
everyone who looks
will see
who we all are!

Eric Chock